Leadership Course

B. Vincent

Published by RWG Publishing, 2021.

LEADERSHIP COURSE

First edition. July 29, 2021.

Written by B. Vincent.

Also by B. Vincent

Bookkeeping
Bridge Pages
Business Acquisition
Business Bogging
Marketing Automation
Better Meetings
Conversion Optimization
Creative Solutions
Employee Recruitment
Startup Capital
Employee Mentoring
Followership
Servant Leadership
Human Resources
Team Building
Freelancing
Funnel Building
Geo Targeting
Goal Setting
Immanent List Building
Lead Generation
Leadership Course
Leadership Transition
LinkedIn Ads
LinkedIn Marketing
Messenger Marketing
New Management
Newsfeed Ads
Search Ads

Leadership Course

John Quincy Adams once said, if your activities move others to dream more, find out additional, accomplish more and become more. You are a pioneer. Administration is ostensibly the absolute most significant worth your association can profit with. In any case, how would we join it into our organizations and into our lives? How would we typify it in the work environment? Also, how would we foster it's difficult in ourselves, yet in everyone around us and beneath us too. Since genuine administration isn't just about creating yourself or overseeing others. It's tied in with affecting positive development and change in individuals you work with. In this course, we're demonstrating how to do precisely that.

So there's an emergency in administration today, maybe one of the best we've at any point confronted. It's all a result of the authority hole. 77% of organizations are at present encountering initiative deficits with that number expected to ascend to 84% in the coming year. So this means the more established age of pioneers at different levels of the organization stepping stool are well, going downhill, they're resigning, they're continuing on, they're kicking the bucket. Also, on account of the segment winter that the created world has been concocting for itself since the 1960s. Those pioneers are not getting traded by more youthful individuals fit for the work. Or on the other hand rather, they may be getting supplanted. However, the pickings sort of thin, in light of the fact that generally, it will be recent college grads filling the holes. What's more, I'm not here to slam recent college grads, however they truly haven't been getting formed into pioneers for the duration of their lives or vocations.

Administration is basically a worth that has been getting disregarded throughout the previous few decades, both in business and in schooling. So in addition to the fact that we have a circumstance where there's a more modest populace of likely pioneers to browse, however the ones who are there don't have the best degree of administration abilities. Indeed, in a new report, 63% of twenty to thirty year olds recognized they haven't been getting the administration advancement they need to confront the test ahead. For every one of the reasons over, an astounding 89% of organization chiefs demand that reinforcing authoritative initiative is a first concern. But then, under 5% of organizations have executed authority advancement at all levels. of the modest number of organizations who do have authority improvement drives, just 10% of leaders feel that those drives obviously affect their organizations. Believe it or not, an incredible 90% believe they're inadequate. To carry this troubling instructions to its decision 56% of organizations are not prepared to meet their administration needs. Furthermore, 71% don't accept their present chiefs are equipped for driving them into what's to come. pretty distressing, isn't that so? Indeed, don't toss the towel in presently. There is some expectation. For organizations that do have full grown administration advancement systems, the quantity of confronting an initiative hole tumbles to simply 49%. Presently let's get straight to the point, that is as yet an emergency. Yet, contrasted with that 77% in all cases we referenced before, that implies that working really hard of creating pioneers can make an organization 45% bound to stay away from the administration hole and emerge from this uncommon emergency perfectly healthy.

So in light of that, how about we plunge into this preparation. Our course will comprise of a progression of basic conversation focuses. These are intended to cover this expansive subject as completely as conceivable to empower development in these imperative regions and to work with a genuine and productive conversation inside your association about how you can each enhance these fundamental attributes both at work and in your own lives. A portion of these will be quite extensive, and a portion of these conversation focuses will be moderately direct and brief. At the finish of this guide comes the main last advance. Conversation time. Try not to avoid this. This is the main piece of this preparation. At the point when you finish this course you need to go through that most un-an hour or something like that going over the inquiries we supply toward the end collectively. Whoever is the big cheese in the gathering should assign a facilitator whose obligation it is that each question is covered and that everybody, time allowing can give their opinion, ensure all commitments are esteemed, all ideas considered, and all feelings regarded. So how about we move into the main conversation point. Show others how its done, successful initiative includes showing not simply telling. Assuming you need your workers to do what you need them to do, then, at that point you should establish the vibe and exhibit how it ought to be finished. Barring yourself from your own principles is a surefire approach to lose your representatives regard and make you unlikable. try to do you say others should do, regardless of whether it's only for straightforward rules, like being proficient or continually being on schedule. Improve constantly. extraordinary pioneers are continually discovering approaches to work on themselves and discover new abilities and regions that they can learn and dominate. You ought to be available to the chances that come your approach to accomplish more noteworthy statures and seek after additional opportunities. Focus on development and continually challenge your group to be better forms of themselves.

Be objective situated. Try not to zero in a lot on the subtleties and consistently remember the higher perspective. Make a rundown of individual group and hierarchical objectives and think of an unequivocal arrangement and technique to accomplish these objectives. Direct your group's concentration and energy into focusing on pressing or critical objectives. These objectives shouldn't be static. All things considered, intermittently assess them to change depending on the situation. Remember that when your objectives and assumptions are unmistakably characterized, your colleagues can all the more likely comprehend the outcome that they're pursuing as a unit. Besides, it's simpler to screen advance and decide disappointments and victories. Assume liability. Genuine pioneers do whatever should be finished. In any case, when things turn out badly, you shouldn't point fingers or look for someone else to take the blame, you should assume liability for your group's activities and decisions and their outcomes. In doing this, you'll show that you're deserving of your group's trust and regard. Regardless, this doesn't imply that awkward or foolish conduct from a colleague ought to be hidden where no one will think to look. It simply implies that when errors occur, you don't allot fault or offer up a substitute. All things being equal, you distinguish the wellspring of the issue. Concoct a game-plan to address the circumstance and keep it from truly happening once more.

Don't miss out!

Visit the website below and you can sign up to receive emails whenever B. Vincent publishes a new book. There's no charge and no obligation.

https://books2read.com/r/B-A-QWUO-AIVQB

BOOKS 2 READ

Connecting independent readers to independent writers.

Also by B. Vincent

Affiliate Marketing
Affiliate Marketing
Affiliate Marketing

Standalone
Business Employee Discipline
Affiliate Recruiting
Business Layoffs & Firings
Business and Entrepreneur Guide
Business Remote Workforce
Career Transition
Project Management
Precision Targeting
Professional Development
Strategic Planning
Content Marketing
Imminent List Building
Getting Past GateKeepers
Banner Ads

Bookkeeping
Bridge Pages
Business Acquisition
Business Bogging
Marketing Automation
Better Meetings
Conversion Optimization
Creative Solutions
Employee Recruitment
Startup Capital
Employee Mentoring
Followership
Servant Leadership
Human Resources
Team Building
Freelancing
Funnel Building
Geo Targeting
Goal Setting
Immanent List Building
Lead Generation
Leadership Course
Leadership Transition
LinkedIn Ads
LinkedIn Marketing
Messenger Marketing
New Management
Newsfeed Ads
Search Ads

About the Publisher

Accepting manuscripts in the most categories. We love to help people get their words available to the world.

Revival Waves of Glory focus is to provide more options to be published. We do traditional paperbacks, hardcovers, audio books and ebooks all over the world. A traditional royalty-based publisher that offers self-publishing options, Revival Waves provides a very author friendly and transparent publishing process, with President Bill Vincent involved in the full process of your book. Send us your manuscript and we will contact you as soon as possible.

Contact: Bill Vincent at rwgpublishing@yahoo.com www.rwgpublishing.com

www.ingramcontent.com/pod-product-compliance
Lightning Source LLC
Chambersburg PA
CBHW030538210326
41597CB00014B/1196